THE EASTER
Swallows

by Vicki Howie

Illustrated by Paola Bertolini Grudina

Two swallows were chattering in a quiet garden.
'It's springtime!' sang Long-tail to his wife. 'Shall we build a nest beside this empty cave?'

'Oh, yes!' said Short-tail. 'We could have a nest full of baby swallows.'

Long-tail nodded his black head.

'And they will have a wonderful view of the great City of Jerusalem! Come along, then! Let's find some mud to build the nest.'

4

The two swallows soared up over the olive trees and down into a muddy field where a donkey was tethered. Backwards and forwards they flew, carrying great globules of mud in their beaks.

As they worked, two men came to fetch the young donkey.

'Where are you going, little donkey?' asked the swallows.

'To carry a great King into Jerusalem,' he brayed. 'I've never given anyone a ride before.'

'Who is this King?' the swallows twittered. 'Shall we go and see?'

The swallows flew to the city gate and joined a crowd of noisy sparrows in a leafy tree.

'Here comes Jesus, our gentle King!' shouted the people down below. 'Look! He's riding on a little donkey.'

'Hurry! Let's cover the dusty road with our cloaks!' called a man.

'But who *is* Jesus?' Short-tail asked the sparrows.

'Jesus is the Son of God!' they chirped. 'He's the one who takes care of all His creatures, even small birds like us!'

'Jesus made my sister well again,' said a boy.

'He told us a lovely story,' added some children who were waving palm branches.

The two swallows watched with bright eyes as Jesus rode towards them. And Short-tail was quite sure that Jesus smiled up at her.

The happy swallows returned to the quiet garden and set to work once more. As the days went by and the muddy nest grew bigger, the swallows listened eagerly to the other birds in the garden chattering about Jesus.

'He saved my life once,' sang a lark. 'A fierce wind blew me out over the stormy lake. But Jesus told the wind and the waves to calm down and I found my way home again.'

'I saw Him feed five thousand hungry people with just five little loaves and two fish,' chirped a sparrow. 'And there were plenty of crumbs left over for us birds.'

'All that work has made *me* hungry,' said Short-tail at last. 'Let's fly over the city walls to find some food.'

The hungry pair soon spotted some breadcrumbs on a window sill. 'Eat up!' said Long-tail to his wife. 'You must keep up your strength!'

But Short-tail was peering through the window into the upstairs room.

'Look! It's our friend Jesus!' she cried happily. 'He's having some supper with His friends!'

Suddenly, one of the men with Jesus left the room and ran down the stone steps.

'That's Judas!' said Long-tail. 'Look at him frowning! I wonder what he's going to do.'

It was getting late now but the two swallows were worried about their friend Jesus. So they followed Him into a garden called Gethsemane that was full of olive trees.

'Please stay awake and keep me company while I pray,' Jesus asked His friends. But they were much too tired and they soon fell asleep.

'*We'll* stay awake with Jesus,' agreed the birds. 'He seems so lonely.'

In the night, Judas brought some Roman soldiers marching into the garden.

'Where is Jesus?' they shouted. 'The one who calls Himself a king.'

'Here I am,' said Jesus. 'But please don't hurt My friends.'

The soldiers took hold of Jesus and marched Him away. Long-tail was angry.

'So *that's* what Judas was doing,' he said. 'I thought he was supposed to be Jesus' friend, but he has betrayed Him.'

Early the next morning, the swallows found Jesus at the palace. A crowd of angry people were shouting.
'Kill Him! Take Him away and put Him on a cross!'
'Why do they want to kill Jesus?' asked Short-tail. 'He hasn't done anything wrong.'
'They don't believe He is the Son of God,' explained Long-tail.

Then the soldiers made a crown out of thorny branches and put it on His head. At this, the swallows flew down to try to lift it off.

But a soldier waved his sword at them and frightened them away.

L ong-tail took Short-tail back to the
    quiet garden.
'You were very brave!' he said proudly.
'But now you must be braver still.'
    Short-tail looked down the path.
The soldiers were making Jesus carry a heavy
cross up the hill. He often slipped and fell.
    'What are they going to do to Jesus?'
she whispered.
    'I'm afraid they are going to kill Him,'
said Long-tail.

That dreadful Friday, the soldiers put Jesus on a cross between two other crosses. They left Him there to die. Then the afternoon sky turned black as night and the ground shook. Long-tail and Short-tail hid their heads under their wings.

'Please forgive them, Father,' Jesus prayed.

And then He died.

'Did you hear that?' asked Short-tail sorrowfully. 'Now they will know that Jesus was a good man!'

In the evening, one of Jesus' friends came to put His body in the cave. Then he rolled a big stone in front of the cave to close it.

'Goodnight,' he said softly to a lady called Mary Magdalene who was crying in the garden.

The swallows sat beside the big stone, feeling very gloomy.

'Don't be sad!' said Long-tail, putting his head on one side.

'But my heart is broken!' replied Short-tail. 'Jesus is dead! Who will look after us now?'

As soon as the stars began to fade on Sunday morning, the swallows woke up and saw that the cave was open. The stone was rolled to one side!

The swallows fluttered inside the cave, but they were surprised to see that it was empty.

'Don't worry!' said an angel. 'Jesus is not dead any more. He's alive!'

The puzzled swallows flew back into the garden. Suddenly it was full of sunshine. Flowers opened their petals and birds began to sing.

Mary was there. But she wasn't crying any more. She was smiling at someone.

'It's Jesus!' exclaimed Long-tail. 'He's alive! He's alive!'

'Oh, Jesus, friend of all the birds, everybody's friend and King, You are alive!' sang Short-tail. 'No one but the Son of God could come back to life again!'

And not long after that, Long-tail and Short-tail were the proud parents of four baby swallows, all opening their beaks for more food in their beautiful Easter nest!

Published 2007 in the UK by CWR, Waverley Abbey House, Waverley Lane, Farnham, Surrey, GU9 8EP, UK. Registered Charity No. 294387. Registered Limited Company No. 1990308. Reprinted 2008.
ISBN: 978-1-85345-416-5

First edition 2007

Editorial Director Annette Reynolds
Art Director Gerald Rogers
Pre-production Krystyna Hewitt
Production John Laister

For a list of CWR's National Distributors visit www.cwr.org.uk/distributors